THE
SHORT TRUNKS'
JOURNEY

Written by Sunshine Orange Studio
Illustrated by Zhou Daling

RC
Books Beyond Boundaries
ROYAL COLLINS

Hi! My name is Cloud, the little one of the Short Trunks. I come from the beautiful Xishuangbanna Prefecture in Yunnan Province. It is a National Nature Reserve in China.

In my hometown, you can see flowers all year round. There are rainforests, and the Lancang River flows across the land. Many Asian elephant herds like ours live there, the Big Lubaos, the Small Ears... We are good neighbors.

Why is our family the Short Trunks? One of our members doesn't have a nose tip, so that's how we are named. We are a big family with a dozen members.

Our life in the Nature Reserve was nice and peaceful. Our number has increased from 170 to 300 within the past forty years. Our human friends also built Asian Elephant Rescue and Breeding Centers to better protect us.

But one day, our matriarch held a family meeting and made an unusual decision: we are going on a trip to the world outside the rain forests.

9

So, we immediately set off. The whole family headed north.

By the way, I was still in my mom's tummy at that time.

The family reached Ning'er County in Pu'er City, and that's where I was born! I had already lived in my mom's tummy for twenty-two months. I was a cute, 100 kg-baby when I came out. It was winter, but Ning'er wasn't cold at all. It was nice and warm.

"One little secret about us:

It is not easy for a baby elephant to come to the world. Elephants have the longest pregnancy among mammals. A mother elephant carries her baby for 20 to 22 months. She will then breast-feed the newborn for three to five years until her next baby is born.

We Asian elephants have a relatively low birth rate. The mothers give birth every six to eight years, and it mostly happens in late fall or early winter. The mother elephants can only have one baby at a time."

Soon after I was born, I could already stand on my own—although not perfectly—and I could travel along with my mom. I was very excited about our journey. I wondered where our destination was.

"Another little secret about us: Newborn elephants weigh between 80 and 120 kg. They are about the same size as calves. They do not yet have very long trunks or tusks. Their skin is brown without any fur. In a few minutes after they are born, they can stand with the help of their mothers. In several hours, they are able to walk and move along with the herd."

We headed north in March 2020. We walked for thousands of kilometers, and our journey covered half of Yunnan Province. Our feet were so big that we often accidentally stepped on flowers and grass as we walked. I felt bad about this, but my mom told me not to worry. We were helping the plants to regenerate more quickly and smaller animals to pass more easily. It felt great to be helpful!

We were warmly received by our human neighbors throughout our journey. I had plantain, tiger grass, corn... and something that tasted really weird. Mom told me that was pineapples.

"I hated pineapples!"

Once, my big brother used his trunk to turn on the tap, and clear water flew out like a stream. So this was what human called running water! There was no silt in it at all. It was so tasty! We all loved it.

We ate a lot, and we pooped a lot. I found it funny that some scientists even took interest in that. My mom told me that our poop would carry many plant seeds to faraway places where they could grow. Our poop actually tells a lot about our bodies. How amazing!

Several times we broke into farmlands by accident. But the people didn't drive us away. The monitors just watched us quietly from a distance.

　　By and by, we became more and more familiar with our human neighbors. This is a very special friendship.

The monitors tracked our movements all the way. They even used drones and IR night vision equipment to record our journey and guide our way.

When it was hot, my family and I would go play in mud puddles and spread mud all over our bodies. Mom said this could protect us from sunburn, keep us hydrated, and help clear the bacteria and parasites off our skin.

It's time to shower again. My mom sucked in a trunkful of water and sprayed me. I was soon cleaned. It was so refreshing after a cool shower.

We have the longest nose among all animals. We can use it to lift very heavy things, to pick up peanuts, or to rub our eyes. Sometimes we will bump each other back and forth. No, we are not fighting. We are just learning how to use our trunks better, because they are very important to us.

Once or twice, I fell into a ditch. I was so scared. But my mom always helped me out with her strong trunk. Lucky me!

We ate and played. When we got tired, we just lay down and slept. My mom could sleep standing, but I had to lie down.

Sometimes, everyone lay down to rest. Because I was the youngest, the adults made me sleep in the middle. I felt very safe with my family around me.

Interestingly, I heard that many of our human friends loved the way we slept together. Do you love it too?

My big brother Tiger is a very spirited young elephant. He always has his own ideas. One day, he suddenly decided to leave us and spend some time on his own. I missed him a lot and I hoped he would come back soon.

Tiger had a great time playing in the
farmland and in the mountains.

But sometimes he got too mischievous, and scientists began to worry about his safety. So they used magic to put him to sleep. When he woke up, he was already back home.

I continued the journey with the rest of the family. We crossed mountains and forests, and we visited villages and cities. These places were very exciting and beautiful, but I still wanted to go back to where we came from. That's our only home.

Finally, on August 8, 2021, we crossed the Yuanjiang River safely. Home was not far ahead. Thank you, our human friends, for protecting us all the way! I love you guys!

It was an amazing journey. We came out of the forests to see the world and let everyone in the world to see us. We live in the same planet with our human neighbors, and we will write a story about us together. I believe it will be a long and beautiful story.

Our Loving and Beloved Land
—the Asian elephant travellers

Written by Li Wei

People say we are immigrants,
Traveling all the way to the north.
But all we want is to look around,
What the world around us is like.
Our hometown is the land of spring,
But there are more exciting views out there,
Waiting to be discovered.

People say we are superstars.
Living under the spotlight.
Thank you for appreciating our cuteness,
We appreciate more of the beauty of the land.
We are in love with the colors,
And we are in love with the men,
Who treat us kindly as friends.

People say we are the royalties,
Enjoying the feast as we wander.
We know that the food is not given as tribute,
But as gifts that represent genuine friendship.
The people of the land,
They greet us "Hi" and bid us "Goodbye."
With care, smiles, and respect,
That's the language we understand.

People say the travelling Short Trunks
are finally back,
To the home they have "abandoned" for so long.
The truth is, we never left, and will never be gone.
We will not forget,
Yunnan, our motherland.
Our loving and beloved land.

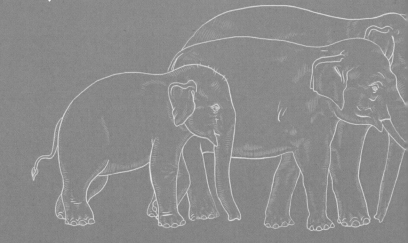

About the author:

Sunshine Orange Studio is composed of professionals engaged in writing, drawing, editing, and typesetting. Over the years, it has planned excellent publications such as *Grandpa Rattan Chair Telling the Ethnic Stories of Yunnan* and *Picture Book of Classical Stories of Yunnan Ethnic Minorities*.

About the illustrator:

Zhou Daling graduated from Yunnan Normal University with a major in Art Design and is working for a well-known design company in Shenzhen. His commercial packaging designs have won many national awards. His illustrations for picture books that are various in styles can be seen in many publications.

The Short Trunks' Journey

Written by Sunshine Orange Studio
Illustrated by Zhou Daling

First published in 2022 by Royal Collins Publishing Group Inc.
Groupe Publication Royal Collins Inc.
BKM Royalcollins Publishers Private Limited

Headquarters: 550-555 boul. René-Lévesque O Montréal (Québec) H2Z1B1 Canada
India office: 805 Hemkunt House, 8th Floor, Rajendra Place, New Delhi 110 008

ISBN: 978-1-4878-0915-7

To find out more about our publications, please visit www.royalcollins.com.